Dolly Parton

Country Music Star

by Kate Moening

BELLWETHER MEDIA • MINNEAPOLIS, MN

Blastoff! Readers are carefully developed by literacy experts to build reading stamina and move students toward fluency by combining standards-based content with developmentally appropriate text.

Level 1 provides the most support through repetition of high-frequency words, light text, predictable sentence patterns, and strong visual support.

Level 2 offers early readers a bit more challenge through varied sentences, increased text load, and text-supportive special features.

Level 3 advances early-fluent readers toward fluency through increased text load, less reliance on photos, advancing concepts, longer sentences, and more complex special features.

★ **Blastoff! Universe**

Reading Level

BLASTOFF! Beginners
Grade **K**

BLASTOFF! READERS
Grades **1-3**

BLASTOFF! DISCOVERY
Grade **4**

This edition first published in 2021 by Bellwether Media, Inc.

No part of this publication may be reproduced in whole or in part without written permission of the publisher. For information regarding permission, write to Bellwether Media, Inc., Attention: Permissions Department, 6012 Blue Circle Drive, Minnetonka, MN 55343.

Library of Congress Cataloging-in-Publication Data

Names: Moening, Kate, author.
Title: Dolly Parton : country music star / by Kate Moening.
Description: Minneapolis : Bellwether Media, 2021. | Series: Women leading the way | Includes bibliographical references and index. | Audience: Ages 5-8 | Audience: Grades K-1 | Summary: "Relevant images match informative text in this introduction to Dolly Parton. Intended for students in kindergarten through third grade"–Provided by publisher.
Identifiers: LCCN 2019053833 (print) | LCCN 2019053834 (ebook) | ISBN 9781644872093 (library binding) | ISBN 9781681038339 (paperback) | ISBN 9781618919670 (ebook)
Subjects: LCSH: Parton, Dolly–Juvenile literature. | Country musicians–United States–Biography–Juvenile literature. | Singers–United States–Biography–Juvenile literature.
Classification: LCC ML3930.P25 M64 2021 (print) | LCC ML3930.P25 (ebook) | DDC 782.421642092 [B]–dc23
LC record available at https://lccn.loc.gov/2019053833
LC ebook record available at https://lccn.loc.gov/2019053834

Text copyright © 2021 by Bellwether Media, Inc. BLASTOFF! READERS and associated logos are trademarks and/or registered trademarks of Bellwether Media, Inc.

Editor: Elizabeth Neuenfeldt   Designer: Andrea Schneider

Printed in the United States of America, North Mankato, MN.

Table of Contents

Who Is Dolly Parton?

Dolly Parton is a country music singer and songwriter. She has written thousands of songs!

Dolly is also an actor, author, and business owner.

Dolly grew up in the **Smoky Mountains** of Tennessee. She had 11 **siblings**!

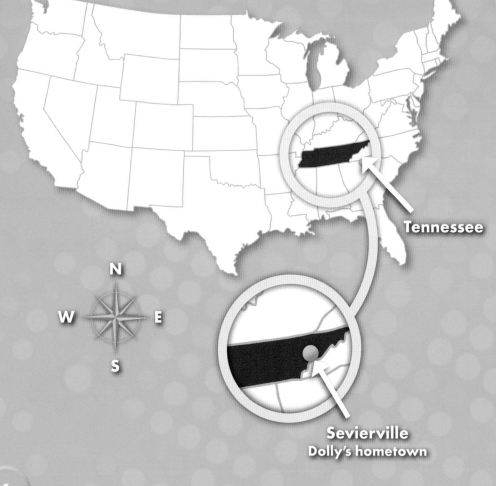

Tennessee

Sevierville
Dolly's hometown

Dolly with her family

The Partons had very little money. But music helped them get through hard times.

Getting Her Start

Dolly started singing when she was five. Her uncle Bill soon gave Dolly her first guitar.

By age 10, she was **performing** on local radio!

Dolly Parton Profile

Birthday: January 19, 1946

Hometown: Sevierville, Tennessee

Field: music

Schooling: high school

Influences:
- Avie Lee Parton (mother)
- Robert Lee Parton (father)
- Porter Wagoner (musician, Dolly's singing partner)

Dolly loved her hometown. But she dreamed of a music **career**.

Dolly moved to Nashville after high school. Many **musicians** have started there!

Nashville

Dolly and her singing partner,
Porter Wagoner, in Nashville

People **connected** to Dolly's songs right away. She won many **awards**.

Her music became
famous around the world!

Dolly singing in England

Dolly's **appearance** made her stand out. Some people did not take her seriously.

But Dolly was proud to be herself. She hoped others would stay true to themselves, too!

"MY DREAM WAS TO **MAKE AS MANY PEOPLE HAPPY** AS I COULD IN THIS LIFE." (2018)

Dolly is more than a musician. In 1980, she started acting in movies!

Dolly acting in a movie in 1980

Dollywood

Dolly also started her own **theme park** called Dollywood. It celebrates the Smoky Mountains.

Dolly's Future

Dolly giving books
to the Library of Congress

Dolly started a **program**
that mails free books to kids.

Today, it has mailed more than 129 million books!

Dolly Parton Timeline

1967 Dolly releases her first album, *Hello, I'm Dolly*

1978 Dolly wins her first Grammy Award for Best Female Country Vocal Performance

1986 Dollywood theme park opens

1995 Dolly starts Imagination Library, which mails books to kids once a month

1999 Dolly is added to the Country Music Hall of Fame

Dolly still writes
music. She has
sold more than
160 million albums.

She **inspires**
artists everywhere.
Dolly wants everyone
to feel proud of who
they are!

"I JUST TRY TO FIND THE GOOD AND THE LIGHT IN EVERY PERSON." (2012)

Glossary

appearance—the way someone or something looks

awards—rewards or prizes given for a job well done

career—a job that someone does for a long time

connected—shared a feeling of understanding

inspires—gives someone an idea about what to do or create

musicians—people who sing, write, or play music

performing—doing an action or activity that requires training and skill

program—a plan of things that are done in order to reach a certain result

siblings—brothers or sisters

Smoky Mountains—a mountain range in North Carolina and Tennessee; the Smoky Mountains are part of the larger Appalachian mountain range.

theme park—an amusement park where the rides or activities are based around a certain idea

To Learn More

AT THE LIBRARY

Parton, Dolly. *Coat of Many Colors*. New York, N.Y.: Grosset & Dunlap, 2016.

Sanchez Vergara, Maria Isabel. *Dolly Parton*. London, U.K.: Lincoln Children's Books, 2019.

Stratton, Connor. *We Make Music*. Lake Elmo, Minn.: Focus Readers, 2020.

ON THE WEB

FACTSURFER

Factsurfer.com gives you a safe, fun way to find more information.

1. Go to www.factsurfer.com.

2. Enter "Dolly Parton" into the search box and click 🔍.

3. Select your book cover to see a list of related content.

Index